W9-CGN-283

snug.

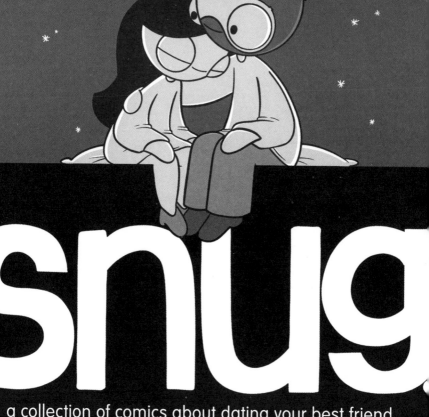

snug

a collection of comics about dating your best friend

Catana Chetwynd

Andrews McMeel
PUBLISHING®

For Nana,
Her Nanliness.
Thank you for giving me my love for art.
And for everything else.

INTRODUCTION

Sometimes, we are so content in our relationship that we don't stop to think about why. It's not *particularly* because of the coffee you shared yesterday, that inside joke you laughed at together, or the kiss you got this morning, but at the same time—it is. There is something so poignantly sentimental about the moments that mean both nothing and everything. And something even more sentimental about these moments being shared between a pair of best friends.

We hope that reading this book brings a smile to your face and maybe even a quick "look" in the direction of your significant other. You know the look I'm talking about.

Remember this book was inspired by you, written for you, and exists because of people like you. We hope you see yourself in it.

So get yourself a coffee, or a glass of wine, or a nice blanket. Get snug. And enjoy this book!

snug.

catana comics

ϵJohn Problemsϵ

does nothing for 3 hours

it's been a lot of talking

21

ordering your girlfriend's coffee

lost in conversation

28

43

reason #174 to love fall
wearing enough layers to hide your food babies

it's like you can't even tell we just ate 6 pounds of mac and cheese

Signs your gf is a sloth

she's a little odd, but very adorable

when i'm cold:

at the grocery store

any time after 9pm

when sock-less

every day from september-may

when he's cold:
that one time 3 years ago

> wow, it's a little chilly out today

when babe's upset

me before you:

me with you:

reasons why i might be stressed

telling a story

earlier

when John makes a driving mistake

when i make a driving mistake

cat:

me:

me as a ghost:

"SUPPORT"

Catana Chetwynd is a self-taught traditional artist and the enthusiastic author of *Catana Comics*. She grew up in Saratoga Springs, New York, where she spent her time creating art and pursuing an education in psychology until accidentally stumbling into the world of comics. Not only is her boyfriend, John, the daily inspiration for her drawings, but he was also the one who suggested a comic series about their relationship in the first place. Thanks to his idea and his inspiring daily antics, Catana was able to pursue her childhood dream of being a cartoonist. She currently lives on the East Coast with John and their tiny, angry dog, Murph.

Andrews McMeel Publishing
a division of Andrews McMeel Universal
1130 Walnut Street, Kansas City, Missouri 64106

www.andrewsmcmeel.com

20 21 22 23 24 SDB 10 9 8 7 6 5 4 3 2 1

ISBN: 978-1-5248-5844-5

Library of Congress Control Number: 2019947292

Editor: Patty Rice
Art Director: Holly Swayne
Production Editor: Amy Strassner
Production Manager: Tamara Haus

Attention: Schools and Businesses
Andrews McMeel books are available at quantity discounts with bulk
purchase for educational, business, or sales promotional use. For information,
please e-mail the Andrews McMeel Publishing Special Sales Department:
specialsales@amuniversal.com.